Dear Annette,
This is your
t

e.

EAV.

8/1/06

FLOWERS FROM
THE TREE OF WISDOM

FLOWERS FROM
THE TREE OF WISDOM

A COLLECTION OF INSPIRING QUOTATIONS

- SECOND EXPANDED EDITION -

GATHERED BY

Eskandar de Vos

joshuabooks.com

Published by:
Joshua Books
P.O. Box 5149, Maroochydore BC
Queensland Australia 4558

All correspondence to the publisher
at the above address.

Distributed by:
Joshua Books
1300 888 221
and
Brumby Books Gemcraft
(03) 9761 5535

ISBN 0 9756878 4 0

Category: Self Help: New Age

Joshua Books

joshuabooks.com

Mankind would lose half its wisdom
built up over centuries
if it lost its great sayings.

- Thomas Jefferson

For my mentor,
Rod.

Contents

Note: Where no author is specified, the author or source of the quote is unknown to the compiler.

Introduction

Inspiring quotations can be a great source of encouragement and strength, and the most memorable ones I have been able to find are contained in this book. Having derived great benefit from these quotations myself, I am delighted to be able to share them with readers.

My initial collection of favourite quotations appeared in the first edition of *Flowers From the Tree of Wisdom*, published in 2003 and reprinted in 2004. Further searching since then has doubled the size of my collection and yielded this second, much expanded edition.

My project of collecting inspiring quotations began a decade ago. At that time I was finding my way back to inner well-being after having gone through a rather problematic period. Having reached its lowest ebb, the tide of my life had turned. It was during that period of recovery that I discovered the joy of reading self-help books. I marvelled at the wise sayings contained in such books, and loved quoting them to friends and family. I was able to repeat many inspiring quotations word perfect, long after I had forgotten where they had come from. Some of the people who heard my quotes came to share my fascination, and a few suggested I should write the best ones down rather than relying on memory. I took this advice and began collecting more systematically.

The day came when I decided to aim at having my collection of quotations published as a book. With this goal in mind, my search became progressively more selective. Only the very best material would qualify for inclusion in my book. Of the many thousands of inspiring quotations that I considered over the years, just over six hundred have found their way into this second edition.

What were the qualities I was looking for? An inspiring quotation - or wise saying, or aphorism - has been aptly described as 'a short sentence based on long experience' (Miguel de Cervantes). It manages, in just a few words, to 'distil a profound truth, a penetrating observation, a heartfelt sermon, a personal philosophy, or a whole system of belief' (Des MacHale). For me, an inspiring quote should convey its message eloquently and succinctly, preferably with a clever touch of wit that grabs our attention and makes it resonate in the mind. If a quote grabbed me in this way, I would grab it back and add it to my collection.

Most of the thoughts underlying the quotations in this book are the common property of humanity as a whole. As Goethe observed, 'All truly wise thoughts have been thought already thousands of times.' The originality of each quotation lies in the wording through which a particular individual has succeeded in expressing one of these universal thoughts.

The quotations presented here were created by other people; all I did was bring them together. My role as compiler is well described in the following words, used by Montaigne in introducing a similar work: 'In this book I have only made up a bunch of other people's flowers, providing of my own only the string to tie them together.' Yet there is, after all, something of myself in this collection, because the choice of what to include has been determined by my own values and interests. The collection reflects my own take on life. As Bergen Evans put it, 'There is wisdom in the selection of wisdom.'

I have grouped the quotes under three broad headings: 'Inspiration and Motivation', 'God and Spirituality', and 'Love and Relationships'. And within each of these groupings, smaller sections are evident; for example, under 'Inspiration and Motivation' are found clusters of quotes on dreams, on leadership, on happiness, and so on. This arrangement makes for a certain coherence and continuity as one reads down the pages. However, readers may prefer to ignore the headings and instead follow de Ligne's advice on how to read a book of aphorisms: 'Open it at random and, having found something that interests you, close the book and meditate.'

My search for inspiring quotes will probably continue indefinitely, because the source appears to be inexhaustible. In any case, the quotes presented here are the best ones I have found so far. My hope is that you will derive as much inspiration and energy from them as I have. I wish you much happiness as you enjoy these flowers gathered from the tree of wisdom.

Eskandar.
Brisbane, 2005.

Inspiration

and

Motivation

Usually the best place to make a new start
is where you are.

- Andrew Matthews

A journey of a thousand miles begins with
a single step.

- Lao Tzu

The person who moves a mountain
begins by carrying away small stones.

- Chinese proverb

How wonderful it is that nobody need wait
a single moment
before starting to improve the world.

- Anne Frank

Begin somewhere; you cannot build a
reputation on what you intend to do.

- Liz Smith

Today is the first day of the rest of your life.

Don't count the days - make the days count.

- Ed Agresta

If you don't think every day is a good day,
just try missing one.

- Cavett Robert

It is not the years in your life
but the life in your years that counts.

- Adlai Stevenson

We have time enough
if we will but use it aright.

- Johann Wolfgang von Goethe

The bad news is time flies.
The good news is you're the pilot.

- Michael Altshuler

Count that day lost whose low descending sun
views from thy hand no worthy action done.

If you do your best in your present moments,
the future takes care of itself.

- Paul Wilson

If you take care of each moment,
you take care of all time.

There is no lack of moments to appreciate,
just a lack of moments we are mindful of.

- Joseph Goldstein & Jack Kornfield

We don't remember days or years;
we remember moments.

- Patrick Lindsay

It is not the past or wake of the ship
that makes it move,
but the movement of the engine
in the present moment.

- Wayne Dyer

It is in your moments of decision
that your destiny is created.

- Anthony Robbins

You are the sum total of all your choices
up until this moment.

- Wayne Dyer

Today is the tomorrow you worried about
yesterday.

- Indian saying

Yesterday is history, tomorrow a mystery.
And today is a gift;
that's why we call it the present.

- Babatunde Olatunji

The past is gone; the future is not yet.
Now I am free from both.

- A Course in Miracles

The future isn't what it used to be.

- Arthur C. Clarke

It takes twenty years to make
an overnight success.

- Eddie Carter

A stone cutter hammering away at a rock may
hit it a hundred times without even a crack
appearing. Then on the hundred-and-first blow
it splits in two. Yet it was not the last blow that
did it, but all that went before.

- Jacob A. Riis

The secret to success is to start from scratch
and keep on scratching.

Determination is like a stamp:
it sticks until it gets to its destination.

- Josh Billings

A determined person is one who,
when they get to the end of their rope,
ties a knot and hangs on.

- Joe L. Griffith

An inventor may try thousands of times
to perfect his invention.
This represents not thousands of failures
but thousands of steps closer to success.

I am not discouraged, because every wrong
attempt discarded is another step forward.

- Thomas Alva Edison

Don't get discouraged.
It's usually the last key in the bunch
that opens the lock.

A quitter never wins, and a winner never quits.

- Napoleon Hill

Failure is success if we learn from it.

- Malcolm S. Forbes

Failure to prepare is preparing to fail.

To try where there is little hope
is to risk failure.
Not to try at all is to guarantee it.

You miss one hundred per cent
of the shots you never take.

- Wayne Gretzky

Being defeated is a temporary condition.
Giving up makes it permanent.

- Marlene von Savant

Our greatest glory is not in never falling,
but in rising every time we fall.

- Confucius

Fall down seven times, get up eight.

- Japanese proverb

The moment of victory is much too short
to live for that and nothing else.

- Khalil Gibran

Out of our private victories,
public victories begin to come.

- Stephen Covey

We will either find a way, or make one.

- Hannibal

Get off the spectators' stand
and on to the field.

Genius is one per cent inspiration
and ninety-nine per cent perspiration.

- Thomas Alva Edison

You will never plough a field
if you only turn it over in your mind.

- Irish proverb

An idea not coupled with action will never
get any bigger than the brain cell it occupied.

- Arnold Glasgow

A mighty flame followeth a tiny spark.

- Dante Alighieri

There is no scarcity of opportunity
to make a living at what you love; there's only
a scarcity of resolve to make it happen.

- Wayne Dyer

The secret of success is
to make your vocation your vacation.

- Mark Twain

Success is a ladder that cannot be climbed
with your hands in your pockets.

- American proverb

It's incredibly easy to get caught up in an
activity trap, in the busy-ness of life,
to work harder and harder at climbing the
ladder of success, only to discover
it's leaning against the wrong wall.

- Stephen Covey

Be sure your feet are planted in the right place before you decide to stand firm.

Be careful what you set your heart on, for it will surely be yours.

- Ralph Waldo Emerson

Where you're headed is more important than how fast you're going.

- Stephen Covey

The only way to discover the limits of the possible is to go beyond them into the impossible.

- Arthur C. Clarke

Argue for your limitations,
and sure enough they are yours.

- Richard Bach

If you keep on saying things are going to be
bad, you have a good chance of being
a prophet.

- Isaac Singer

Whether you think you can
or you think you can't, you are right.

- Henry Ford

If my mind can conceive it,
and my heart can believe it,
I know I can achieve it.

- Jesse Jackson

Believe that life is worth living
and your belief will help create the fact.

- William James

The purpose of life is to live a life of purpose.

- Richard Leider

Have purpose that will outlive you.

- Denis Waitley

The most important thing about goals
is to have one.

- Geoffrey F. Abert

A man without a goal
is like a boat without a rudder.

- Thomas Carlyle

The tragedy of life does not lie in
not reaching your goals;
the tragedy lies in not having any goals
to reach.

- Benjamin I. Mays

Find an aim in life
before you run out of ammunition.

Obstacles are those frightful things you see
when you take your eyes off the goal.

- Henry Ford

Focus your mind with great, positive intention.
A laser beam is so focused
that it can burn holes in metal.
Be just as focused on your goal.

Make your life a mission - not an intermission.

- Arnold Glasgow

Some people think and say 'why?'
Others dream and say 'why not?'

- George Bernard Shaw

Nothing happens unless first a dream.

- Carl Sandburg

The future belongs to those who believe
in the beauty of their dreams.

- Eleanor Roosevelt

Dreams come true; without that possibility,
nature would not make us have them.

- John Updike

Those who dream the most do the most.

- Indian saying

Dreams come a size too big
so that we can grow into them.

- Langston Hughes

Never give up on a dream just because of the
time it will take to accomplish it.
The time will pass anyway.

You must go through the nightmare
before the dream is complete.

If one dream should fail
and break into a thousand pieces,
never be afraid to pick one of those pieces up
and begin again.

- Flavia Weeden

Dream the dreams
that have never been dreamt.

- David Bower

The best way to make your dreams come true
is to wake up.

- Paul Valery

If you think that something small cannot
make a difference, try going to sleep
with a mosquito in the room.

- 14th Dalai Lama

An old man was walking along a beach where
thousands of starfish had washed ashore.
Further on he saw a girl picking up the
starfish, one by one, and tossing them back
into the ocean. Approaching her he said,
'Silly girl! There are thousands of starfish here.
How can your little effort possibly
make any difference?'
Smiling and tossing another starfish into the
sea, the girl replied,
'It makes a difference to this one.'

Never turn a job down because you think it's
too small; you don't know where it could lead.

- Julia Morgan

Why not go out on a limb?
That's where the fruit is.

- Will Rogers

We cannot discover new oceans until we have
the courage to lose sight of the shore.

- Andre Gide

The Extra Mile will have no traffic jams.

Be governed by your internal compass,
not by some clock on the wall.

- Stephen Covey

Either control your own destiny,
or someone else will!

- John F. Welch, Jr.

Believe in yourself
and others will believe in you as well.

You cannot go any higher than your
self image.

- John C. Maxwell

No one can make you inferior
without your consent.

- Eleanor Roosevelt

No one can drive us crazy
unless we give them the keys.

- Doug Horton

Things turn out the best for those who make
the best out of the way things turn out.

- Art Linkletter

We cannot direct the wind,
but we can adjust the sails.

The wind and the waves are always on the side
of the ablest navigators.

- Edward Gibbon

Luck is the meeting of
preparation and opportunity.

- Vince Lombardi

I am a great believer in luck, and I find the
harder I work the more I have of it.

- Thomas Jefferson

No one ever stumbled across anything
sitting down.

- Charles Kettering

Even if you're on the right track,
you'll get run over if you just sit there.

- Will Rogers

The block of granite which is an obstacle
in the pathway of the weak becomes
a stepping-stone in the pathway of the strong.

- Thomas Carlyle

A bend in the road is not the end of the
road ... unless you fail to make the turn.

The road to success in life is lined with
many tempting parking spaces.

The road to success is always under
construction.

- Mary O'Hare Dumas

Our five senses are incomplete without the
sixth - a sense of humour.

God gave us two ends,
one to sit on and one to think with.
Success depends on which one you use:
heads, you win; tails, you lose.

The quickest way to double your money is to
fold it in half and put it back in your pocket.

- Will Rogers

If you lend someone twenty dollars,
and never see that person again,
it was probably worth the money.

Even a mosquito doesn't get a pat on the back
until he is well into his work.

Never test the depth of the water with
both feet.

The trouble with the rat-race is that
even if you win, you are still a rat.

- Lily Tomlin

Always remember you are unique,
just like everyone else.

- Alison Boulter

All my life I've wanted to be someone;
I guess I should have been more specific.

- Jane Wagner

A celebrity is someone who is known
merely for being well known.

- Daniel J. Boorstin

A bore is a man who,
when you ask him how he is, tells you.

- Bert Leston Taylor

Just because I have pain,
doesn't mean I have to be one.

Blessed are they who can
laugh at themselves,
for they shall never cease to be amused.

- John Powell

I think the next best thing to solving a
problem is finding some humour in it.

- Frank Clark

I hope life isn't a big joke ...
because I don't get it.

- Jack Handey

If you're not doing something with your life,
it doesn't matter how long it is.

- Peace Corps commercial

If the going is easy, beware.
You may be headed downhill.

If you think you're tops,
you won't do much climbing.

Don't let the best you have done so far be the
standard for the rest of your life.

- Gustavus F. Swift

Hold yourself responsible for a higher
standard than anybody else expects of you.

- Henry Ward Beecher

The greatest revenge in life is
doing what others say you cannot.

- Walter Bagehot

Man who says 'It cannot be done' should not interrupt man who is doing it.

- Chinese proverb

People are always ready to admit a man's ability after he gets there.

- Bob Edwards

Never criticise something that you are not willing to do yourself.

- David Baird

A successful person is one who can lay a firm foundation with the bricks that others throw at him or her.

- David Brinkley

No matter how people react to me,
I know I am a worthwhile person.

- Susan Jeffers

We may not be perfect,
but some parts of us are excellent.

Excellence is the pursuit of perfection,
not the attainment.

We are what we repeatedly do.
Excellence, then, is not an act; it is a habit.

- Aristotle

Give me a lever long enough
and a prop strong enough,
and I can single-handedly move the world.

- Archimedes

Nothing splendid has ever been achieved except
by those who dared believe that something
inside of them was superior to circumstance.

- Bruce Barton

We are not creatures of circumstance;
we are creators of circumstance.

- Benjamin Disraeli

I saw the angel in the marble
and carved until I set him free.

- Michelangelo

Vision is the art of seeing things invisible.

- Jonathan Swift

The most pathetic person in the world is
someone who has sight but has no vision.

- Helen Keller

If vision doesn't cost you something,
it's a daydream.

- John C. Maxwell

Vision is like seeing the picture
on the box cover
when putting together a jigsaw puzzle.

- James Kouzes & Barry Posner

There is a law in psychology that if you form a
picture in your mind of what you would like to
be, and you keep and hold that picture there
long enough, you will soon become exactly as
you have been thinking.

- William James

Treat yourself as if you already are
what you'd like to be.

- Hassidic saying

Nothing great will ever be achieved without
great men, and men are great only if they are
determined to be so.

- Charles de Gaulle

Leaders are ordinary people
with extraordinary determination.

Good leaders must first become good servants.

- *Robert Greenleaf*

He who has never learned to obey
cannot be a good commander.

- *Aristotle*

The leader is the chief servant of the tribe.

- *Mohammed*

Leaders must be close enough
to relate to others,
but far enough ahead to motivate them.

- *John C. Maxwell*

A good leader inspires people
to have confidence in him;
a great leader inspires them
to have confidence in themselves.

It's always good when followers believe in their
leaders, but it is even better when leaders
believe in their followers.

- Mardy Grothe

If you are not afraid to face the music,
you may some day lead the band.

- Spuk Tiding

A man who wants to lead the orchestra
must turn his back on the crowd.

- James Crook

Follow the crowd and you will never be
followed by a crowd.

No one can give you authority.
But if you act like you have it,
others will believe you do.

- Karin Ireland

Strengthen me so that the power of my example
will far exceed the authority of my rank.

- Pauline H. Peters

I don't know any other way to lead
but by example.

Today a reader - tomorrow a leader.

- W. Fusselman

Life is like a dogsled team. If you ain't
the lead dog, the scenery never changes.

- Lewis Grizzard

If a man does not keep pace with his
companions, perhaps it is because he hears
the beat of a different drummer.
Let him step to the music he hears,
however measured or far away.

- Henry David Thoreau

Do not seek to follow in the footsteps
of the wise. Seek what they sought.

- Basho

Do not follow where the path may lead.
Go instead where there is no path
and leave a trail.

- Ralph Waldo Emerson

Two roads diverged in a wood, and I -
I took the one less travelled by,
and that has made all the difference.

- Robert Frost

Will you be the rock
that redirects the course of the river?

- Claire Nuer

Great spirits have always encountered
violent opposition from mediocre minds.

- Albert Einstein

Each player must accept the cards life
deals him. But once they are in hand,
he alone must decide how to play the cards
in order to win the game.

- Voltaire

Life is not a matter of holding good cards,
but playing a poor hand well.

- Robert Louis Stevenson

For most of your life
you've lived the effect of your experiences.
Now you're invited to be the cause of them.

- Neale D. Walsch

Life is what is happening
while you are making other plans.

- John Lennon

The more sand that has escaped
from the hourglass of our life,
the clearer we should see through it.

- Jean Paul

Life is a process of
continual re-evaluation and growth;
just as a lawn may be immaculately mown,
yet weeds begin to grow and problems arise.

Don't just go through life. Grow through life.

- Eric Butterworth

Life is like riding a bicycle. You don't fall off
unless you plan to stop pedalling.

Progress is a tide.
If we stand still, we will surely be drowned.
To stay on the crest we have to keep moving.

- Harold Mayfield

The lowest ebb is the turn of the tide.

Whatever happens in life, if it doesn't kill you,
it can only make you stronger.

- Johann Wolfgang von Goethe

I am enrolled in the University of Life.

- Stephen Lin

Give a man a fish, and he eats for a day.
Teach a man to fish,
and he eats for a lifetime.

- Chinese proverb

When the student is ready,
the teacher will appear.

- Zen proverb

The least likely teacher might offer you
the most to learn.

- Brian Beirne

I have never met a man so ignorant
that I couldn't learn something from him.

- Galileo Galilei

If a drunkard lying in the gutter says
'Don't drink!' he is giving valuable advice
even though he is not following it himself.

- Chao Chuen

When I was a boy of fourteen, my father was so
ignorant I could hardly stand to have the old
man around. But, when I got to be twenty-one,
I was astonished at how much the old man had
learned in only seven years.

- Mark Twain

We are here to learn lessons, and the world is
our teacher. When we fail to learn a lesson, we
get to take it again ... and again! Once we have
learned the lesson, we move on to the next one.
(And we never run out of lessons!)

- Andrew Matthews

Experience is a hard teacher,
because she gives the test first,
the lesson afterward.

- Vernon Law

Experience is something you don't get until
just after you need it.

A moment's insight is sometimes worth
a life's experience.

- Oliver Wendell Holmes

Experience is the name everyone gives
to their mistakes.

- Oscar Wilde

Learn from the mistakes of others.
You can't live long enough
to make them all yourself.

- Sam Levinson

Anyone who has made a mistake and doesn't
correct it, is making another one.

- Confucius

The greatest mistake in life is
to be continually fearing you will make one.

- Elbert Hubbard

Admit you're wrong when you're wrong,
and you'll be right.

There is no wrong time to do the right thing.

- David Baird

It is never too late to be
what you might have been.

- George Eliot

Courage is not the absence of fear
but the mastery of fear.

- Mark Twain

Courage is the art of being the only one
who knows you're scared to death.

- Earl Wilson

It's all right to have butterflies in your stomach.
Just get them to fly in formation.

- *Rob Gilbert*

Feel the fear, and do it anyway.

- *Susan Jeffers*

FEAR means
False **E**vidence **A**ppearing **R**eal.
Or
False **E**motion **A**ppearing **R**eal.

- *Anthony Robbins*

We must tackle the fascinating problem of how
to control the harmful aspects of fear response
while retaining its protective benefits.

- *Stewart Agras*

A man who fears suffering
is already suffering from what he fears.

- Michel de Montaigne

There is nothing to fear but fear itself.

- Franklin D. Roosevelt

Worry is like a rocking chair.
It gives you something to do
but it doesn't get you anywhere.

- Evan Esar

The more we worry, the more we have
something to worry about.

- Tom Seeley

The time to relax is
when you don't have time for it.

- Sydney J. Harris

My schedule is so full,
I do not have time for crises.

A crisis event often explodes the illusions
that anchor our lives.

- Robert L. Veninga

People are like stained glass windows.
They sparkle and shine when the sun is out,
but when the darkness sets in, their true beauty
is revealed only if there is a light from within.

- Elizabeth Kubler Ross

In times of storm,
the depth of the root structure is revealed.

We're like tea bags. We don't know our
strength until we get into hot water.

- Bruce Laingen

Whenever you need to know about
the unconscious part in you,
the challenges of the present will bring it out.

- Eckhart Tolle

It is not because things are difficult that we do
not dare; it is because we do not dare
that they are difficult.

- Seneca

Most of our regrets relate to things that we
didn't do rather than to what we have done.

Please remember, the greatest troubles you have
to face are those that never come.

- Dr. Greatheart

These days, one is exhausted more from
the task ahead than the task at hand.

- Jonar C. Nader

Achieve a balance
between being and becoming,
or between striving and arriving.

It is good to have an end to journey towards,
but it is the journey that matters in the end.

- Ursula K. Le Guin

In the long run the pessimist
may be proved right,
but the optimist has a better time on the trip.

- Daniel L. Reardon

It's not doing what you like that's important -
it's liking what you do.

- Eric Butterworth

To be upset over what you don't have ...
is to waste what you do have.

- Ken Keyes

When you can't have what you want,
it's time to start wanting what you have.

- Kathleen A. Sutton

To be without some of the things you want
is an indispensable part of happiness.

- Bertrand Russell

There is no way to happiness;
happiness is the way.

- Wayne Dyer

If you want to live a happy life, tie it to a goal -
not to people or things.

- Albert Einstein

Happiness is a butterfly which, when pursued,
is always just beyond your grasp,
but if you sit down quietly,
may alight upon you.

- *Nathaniel Hawthorne*

If you ever find happiness by hunting for it,
you will find it, as the old woman did her lost
spectacles, safe on her nose all the time.

- *Josh Billings*

Now and then it's good to pause in our pursuit
of happiness and just be happy.

- *Guillaume Apollinaire*

Most people are about as happy
as they make their minds up to be.

- *Abraham Lincoln*

A happy person is not a person
in a certain set of circumstances,
but rather a person
with a certain set of attitudes.

- Hugh Downs

If you have an attitude you want to keep,
write it in concrete, not sand.

- Anthony Robbins

The state of your life is nothing more than a
reflection of your state of mind.

- Wayne Dyer

Keep your face to the sunshine
and you cannot see the shadows.

- Helen Keller

Recovery lies in repeated doing
until the memory of enough achievement
replaces defeatist contemplation.

- Claire Weeks

The beginning of a habit is like an invisible
thread, but every time we repeat the act we
strengthen the strand, add to it another filament,
until it becomes a great cable and binds us
irrevocably in thought and act.

- Orison Marden

Watch your thoughts; they become your words.
Watch your words; they become your actions.
Watch your actions; they become your habits.
Watch your habits; they become your character.
Watch your character,
for it will become your destiny.

- Rabbi Hillel

Reputation is what people think you are;
character is who you really are.
Take care of your character
and your reputation will take care of itself.

How a man plays the game shows
something of his character;
how he loses shows all of it.

Winning is nice if you don't
lose your integrity in the process.

- Arnold Horshak

No man can wear one face to himself and
another to the multitude without finally getting
bewildered as to which may be true.

- Nathaniel Hawthorne

He who trims himself to suit everyone
will soon whittle himself away.

- Raymond Hull

Judge a man not by how he treats his equals
but by how he treats his inferiors.

Always treat your employees exactly as
you want them to treat your best customers.

- Stephen Covey

It's easier to fight for one's principles
than to live up to them.

- Alfred Alder

The ancestor to every action is a thought.

- Ralph Waldo Emerson

Your mind can only hold one thought at a time,
so make it a positive and constructive one.

- H. Jackson Brown Jr.

As long as you're going to think anyway,
think big.

- Donald Trump

What you focus on expands ...
so think about what you want!

- Andrew Matthews

There are no menial jobs, only menial attitudes.

- William J. Bennet

Who is rich?
He that rejoices in his portion.

- Benjamin Franklin

Some people walk in the rain.
Others just get wet.

- Roger Miller

Change your demands to preferences.

- Ken Keyes

It is better to light one candle
than to curse the darkness.

- Confucius

Instead of being *against* something,
be *for* something.

- Wayne Dyer

Remember that when you
point a finger at someone,
three fingers are pointing back at you.

Responsibility means
to 'respond' with 'ability'.

- Stephen Covey

You are the only one who can use your ability.
It is an awesome responsibility.

- Zig Ziglar

It's not what you've got;
it's what you use that makes a difference.

- Zig Ziglar

He that is good at making excuses
is seldom good at anything else.

- Benjamin Franklin

Not being able to do everything is no excuse for
not doing everything you can.

- Ashleigh Brilliant

Our chief want in life is someone who will
make us do what we can.

- Ralph Waldo Emerson

There is no heavier burden
than a great potential.

- Charlie Brown

The only honest measure of your success
is what you are doing
compared with your true potential.

- Paul J. Meyer

Everyone is gifted; it's just that some
leave the wrapping on longer than others.

How old would you be
if you didn't know how old you were?

- Satchel Paige

We don't stop playing because we get old;
we grow old because we stop playing.

- George Bernard Shaw

Don't think of retiring from the world
until it will be sorry that you retire.

- Samuel Johnson

Here is the test to find whether your mission
on earth is finished: If you're alive, it isn't.

- Richard Bach

God

and

Spirituality

People see God every day,
they just don't recognise him.

- Pearl J. Bailey

The amazing and incomprehensible fact is
not that you can become conscious of God
but that you are not conscious of God.

- Eckhart Tolle

If you can't see God in all,
you can't see God at all.

- Yogi Bhajan

If you can find the God inside of yourself,
you can find the God inside everybody.

- Stephen Levine

It is not called finding God because
how can you find that which was never lost,
the very life that you are.

- Eckhart Tolle

If God is your target, you're in luck,
because God is so big you can't miss.

- Neale D. Walsch

It is difficult to know why God reveals himself
to some and plays the game of hide and seek
with others.

- Papa Ramdas

An atheist is God playing hide and seek
with himself.

- Stanislav Grof

God's first language is silence;
everything else is a bad translation.

- Peter O. Erbe

To hear God's voice
turn down the world's volume.

Be still and know that I am God.

- Psalm 46:10

If you saw yourself as God sees you,
you would smile a lot.

The eye with which I see God is the same eye
by which God sees me.

- Meister Eckhart

God is closer to me than I am to myself.

Your relationship to people is
your relationship to God.

We are as near to God as we are
to the person we least like.

When you realise God,
you realise how human you are.

We are the pencil in God's hand.

We are all the temple of the living God.

- II Corinthians 6:16

Your talent is God's gift to you.
What you do with it is your gift back to God.

- Eleanor Powell

One night, in a dream, I looked back on my life,
and saw two sets of footprints in the sand.
One was mine and one was the Lord's.
However, I noticed that in the lowest and
saddest times there was only one set,
and I asked the Lord why.
He said, 'My precious child,
that was when I was carrying you.'

Let go, let God.

God, it is today that I am free
because my will is yours.

- A Course in Miracles

Only God himself is free,
in the special sense that he is not determined
by anything outside himself.

- John Hick

If God is absolutely everything,
then God desires and wants
absolutely nothing.

- Neale D. Walsch

God sends the rain
on the just and the unjust alike.

- Matthew 5:45

Never think that God's delays
are God's denials.
A lone shipwreck survivor built a hut
and placed in it all he had salvaged.
He prayed to God and scanned the horizon
each day to hail any passing ship.
One day his hut burnt down. He cursed God.
Yet the very next day, a ship arrived.
'We saw your smoke signal,' the captain said.

- Walter A. Heiby

All things are possible with God.

- Mark 10:27

God brings into existence
things that never were.

- Romans 4:17

The universe is a molecule in the body of God.

- Neale D. Walsch

Anyone can count the seeds in an apple,
but only God
can count all the apples in one seed.

- Robert H. Schuller

I know not what the future holds,
but I know Who holds the future.

History is His story.

To everything there is a season,
a time for every purpose under the sun.

- Ecclesiastes 3:1

Time is what keeps the light from reaching us.
There is no greater obstacle to God than time.

- Meister Eckhart

Time is God's way of keeping everything
from happening at once.

A watch implies a watch-maker,
and a universe implies a God.

All that I have seen teaches me
to trust the Creator for all I have not seen.

- Ralph Waldo Emerson

If you trust in yourself,
you trust in the wisdom that created you.

- Wayne Dyer

You cannot know the meaning of your life
until you are consciously connected
to the power that created you.

- Shri Mataji Nirmala Devi

Prayer makes your heart bigger,
until it is capable of containing
the gift of God himself.

- Mother Teresa

Ask and you will receive.
Seek and you will find.
Knock, and it will be opened to you.

- Matthew 7:7

Pray not for gain but for joy
at the opening of the flowers in spring.

True prayer is asking God what He wants.

- William Barclay

Prayer is speaking to God;
meditation is listening.

- Shirley MacLaine

When life knocks you down to your knees,
you are in a perfect position to pray.

Reach up as far as you can,
and God will reach down all the way.

Pray as if it all depends on God,
but work as if it all depends upon you.

- George W. Carver

When life presents more challenges than
you can handle, delegate to God.
He not only *has* the answer; He *is* the answer.

- Tavis Smiley

Don't tell God how big your problems are ...
Tell your problems how big God is.

If the only prayer you said in your whole life
was 'thank you', that would suffice.

- Meister Eckhart

Lord, make me an instrument of thy peace.
Where there is hatred, let me sow love;
Where there is injury, pardon;
Where there is doubt, faith;
Where there is despair, hope;
Where there is darkness, light;
Where there is sadness, joy ...
For it is in giving that we receive.

- Francis of Assisi

What on earth are you doing for Heaven's sake?

Christ is not valued at all
unless he is valued above all.

- Augustine of Hippo

Each of us is an innkeeper who decides
whether there is room for Jesus.

- Neal A. Maxwell

I have been all things unholy.
If God can work through me,
he can work through anyone.

- Francis of Assisi

We are not punished for our sins, but by them.

- Elbert Hubbard

The saints are the sinners who keep on trying.

- Robert Louis Stevenson

True nobility is not about
being better than anyone else.
It is about being better than you used to be.

- Wayne Dyer

True humility: not thinking less of ourselves,
but thinking of ourselves less.

- Rick Warren

My religion is very simple;
my religion is kindness.

- 14th Dalai Lama

Each person must learn
to respect the other's religion.

- John Paul II

God is too big to fit into just one religion.

We are not human beings
having a spiritual experience;
we are spiritual beings
having a human experience.

- Pierre Teilhard de Chardin

You are here to enable
the divine purpose of the universe to unfold.
That is how important you are.

- Eckhart Tolle

There is only one corner of the universe
you can be certain of improving,
and that's your own self.

- Aldous Huxley

What is in front of you and what is behind you
is nothing compared with
what is inside you.

- Ralph Waldo Emerson

You must have a room,
or a certain hour or so a day,
where you don't know what was in the
newspaper that morning ...
a place where you can simply experience and
bring forth what you are and what you might be.

- Joseph Campbell

Solitude can be frightening
because it invites us to meet a stranger
we think we may not want to know -
ourselves.

- Melvyn Kinder

The most difficult relationship you will ever be
in is the one with yourself.
It's the one you can't walk out of.

You might as well learn to like yourself;
you have an awful lot of time
to spend with you.

The foolish want to conquer the world.
The wise want to conquer themselves.

- John C. Maxwell

The longest journey you will make is
from your head to your heart.
We are all on this journey.

- Gary Zukav

The heart has its reasons
that reason does not know.

- Blaise Pascal

It is only with the heart that one can see rightly;
what is essential is invisible to the eye.

- Antoine de Saint-Exupery

The life which is unexamined
is not worth living.

- Plato

Observe all men; thyself most.

- Poor Richard's Almanac

Easily seen are others' faults.
Hard to see are one's own.

- The Buddha

I dreamed death came the other night,
And heaven's gate swung wide.
With kindly grace an angel fair
Ushered me inside.
And there to my astonishment
Stood folks I'd known on earth.
Some I'd judged and labelled as
Unfit, of little worth.
Indignant words rose to my lips,
But never were set free,
For every face showed stunned surprise:
No one expected me!

No one can cheat anyone except himself.

- David Baird

This above all: to thine own self be true.

- William Shakespeare

Life is not a problem to be solved
but a mystery to be lived.

- Van Kaam

A bird doesn't sing because it has an answer;
it sings because it has a song.

- Maya Angelou

One of the diseases to afflict this century
is a loss of wonder.
We cannot revere creation
if we have lost our wonder about it.

- Madeleine L'Engle

If the doors of perception were cleansed,
everything would appear to man as it is:
infinite.

- William Blake

To see the world in a grain of sand
and heaven in a wildflower;
to hold infinity in the palm of your hand,
and eternity in an hour.

- William Blake

The moment one gives close attention to
anything, even a blade of grass,
it becomes a mysterious, awesome,
indescribably magnificent world in itself.

- Henry Miller

Why stay in a five-star hotel,
when you can go camping and experience
more stars than you can count.

- Choong Mun-keat

Money will buy a bed, but not sleep;
Books, but not brains;
Food, but not appetite;
A house, but not a home;
Medicine, but not health;
Luxuries, but not culture;
Amusement, but not happiness;
Religion, but not salvation;
A passport to everywhere but heaven.

Health is wealth.

The most important things in life aren't things.

You may possess things,
but you must not be possessed by them.

- Aurobindo

If your house is your most important
possession, then it is your prison.
Your house should be a hostel you happen to
stay in day after day.

- Robert Allen

We don't need more to be thankful for;
we just need to be more thankful.

Persons thankful for little things are certain to
be the ones with much to be thankful for.

- Frank Clark

Abundance is not something we acquire.
It is something we tune in to.

- Wayne Dyer

A crust eaten in peace is better
than a banquet partaken in anxiety.

- Aesop

Know God, Know Peace.
No God, No Peace.

- Indian saying

The fruit of love is service;
The fruit of service is peace.

- Mother Teresa

If you are wondering
whether or not to do something,
use peace as the criterion.

- Wayne Dyer

Nothing can bring you peace but yourself.

- Ralph Waldo Emerson

When you know yourself, there is peace.

When my heart is at peace,
the world is at peace.

- Chinese proverb

Peace is not the absence of war;
it is a virtue, a state of mind, a disposition
for benevolence, confidence, and justice.

- Baruch Spinoza

Peace is not made at the council table or by
treaties, but in the hearts of men.

- Herbert Clark Hoover

We can never obtain peace in the world
if we neglect the inner world
and don't make peace with ourselves.
World peace must develop out of inner peace.

- 14th Dalai Lama

When the power of love overcomes the love of
power, the world will know peace.

- Jimi Hendrix

If you want to make peace,
you don't talk to your friends.
You talk to your enemies.

- Moshe Dayan

The love of one's country is a splendid thing.
But why should love stop at the border?

- Pablo Casals

A man's feet should be planted in his country,
but his eyes should survey the world.

- George Santayana

The crisis is in our consciousness,
not in the world.

- J. Krishnamurti

Our scientific power
has outrun our spiritual power.
We have guided missiles and misguided men.

- Martin Luther King

The significant problems we face today
cannot be solved at the same level of thinking
we were at when we created them.

- Albert Einstein

Although the world is full of suffering,
it is full also of the overcoming of it.

- Helen Keller

We are healed of suffering only by
experiencing it to the full.

- Marcel Proust

The best way out of emotional pain
is through it.

If you're going through hell, keep going.

- Winston Churchill

You can't drown your sorrows;
they always float to the surface.

It is not my pain but *the* pain.
It is not my problem but *the* problem.

Physical strength is measured
by what we can carry,
spiritual strength by what we can bear.

God gives every bird his worm,
but he doesn't throw it into the nest.

- Swedish proverb

Every flower must grow through dirt.

Patience is never more important than
when you are on the verge of losing it.

Infinite patience brings immediate results.

- Wayne Dyer

Angels fly because
they take themselves lightly.

- G. K. Chesterton

All emotions are pure which
gather you and lift you up.
That emotion is impure which seizes only
one side of your being and so distorts you.

- Rainer Maria Rilke

EMOTION is Energy in MOTION.

The soul that sees beauty
may sometimes walk alone.

- Johann Wolfgang von Goethe

Give me beauty in the inward soul.
May the outward and the inward man be at one.

- Socrates

Your eyes are the window to your soul.

The body is the house to the soul.

Once your mind is stretched to a new
dimension, it never returns.

- Oliver Wendell Holmes

An open mind is like an open mouth
and must be kept open until it finds
something solid upon which to close.

- G. K. Chesterton

Minds, like parachutes,
work only when they are open.

- Thomas Dewar

Have a mind that is open to everything
and attached to nothing.

- Wayne Dyer

A belief is not merely an idea that the mind possesses; it is an idea that possesses the mind.

- Robert Bolton

The mind is its own place, and in itself can make a Heaven of Hell, and a Hell of Heaven.

- John Milton

The choice is up to you.
It can either be 'Good morning, God!' or
'Good God - morning!'

- Wayne Dyer

Some people grumble because
roses have thorns.
I am thankful that thorns have roses.

- Alphonse Karr

We don't see things as they are;
we see them as we are.

- Anais Nin

What you see depends on
what you're looking for.

What is in the inner recesses of the mind
is reflected in the external world.

Nothing has meaning or value other than
the meaning and value that you give it.

Change the way you look at things,
and the things you look at change.

- Wayne Dyer

Change your thoughts
and you change your world.

- Norman Vincent Peale

As you think so shall you be.

A man is not what he thinks he is;
but what he thinks, he is.

- Max R. Hickerson

Your thoughts are slippery as eels.
Just watch how they dart
through the waters of the mind.

- Robert Allen

The mind has a mind of its own.

The feeling of an 'I' distinct from experience is
brought about by memory and the rapidity with
which thoughts follow one another.

There is no self-entity separate
from the flow of experience.

- *The Buddha*

As the arrow-maker carves
and makes straight his arrows,
so the master directs his straying thoughts.

- *The Buddha*

Just as, when the surface of a lake is calm,
you can see right to the bottom,
so also with a calm mind you can have insight.

- *The Buddha*

The quieter you become, the more you can hear.

When you become quiet, it just dawns on you.

When confusion ceases, tranquillity comes;
when tranquillity comes, wisdom appears;
and when wisdom appears, reality is seen.

- Keizan Jokan

Intuition is born of a focused mind.

What we are looking for is who is looking.

- Francis of Assisi

As the mind watches its own movements with
full awareness, there comes the realisation that
the observer is the observed,
the thinker is the thought.

- J. Krishnamurti

The observer observes itself
and becomes the observed.
The seer sees itself and becomes the scenery.

- Deepak Chopra

Two birds, inseparable companions,
perch on the same tree.
One eats the fruit, the other looks on.
The first bird is our individual self, feeding on
the pleasures and pains of this world;
the other is the universal Self,
silently witnessing all.

- Mundaka Upanishad

A real voyage of discovery
consists not in seeking new landscapes
but in having new eyes.

- Marcel Proust

You find in solitude only what you take to it.

- Juan R. Jimenez

The only Zen you find on the tops of the
mountains is the Zen you bring up there.

- Robert Pirsig

Two Zen monks came to a river,
which a young woman was wanting to cross.
One of the monks carried her across.
Later the other monk asked why he broke the
rules by touching a woman.
He replied: 'Are you still carrying her?
I put her down on the river bank!'

- Zen story

If a man rowing across a river
collides with an empty boat,
he does not become very angry.
But if there is someone in the other boat,
he curses him angrily.
Therefore empty your own boat
and no-one will oppose you.

- Chuang Tzu

Have you ever noticed a calm person
with a loud voice?

- Paul Wilson

Zen masters often hit their pupils.
When life smacks you across the head,
bow and say, 'Thank you.'

- Robert Allen

Before enlightenment:
chopping wood, carrying water.
After enlightenment:
chopping wood, carrying water.

- Zen saying

Who looks outside dreams;
who looks inside awakens.

- Carl Jung

Last night I dreamt I was a butterfly ...
Suddenly I awoke ...
Now I do not know whether I was then
a man dreaming I was a butterfly,
or whether I am now
a butterfly dreaming that I am a man.

- Chuang Tzu

Just as we see, on awakening in the morning,
that our dream during the night was unreal,
so we will see, on attaining the meditative
awakening, that our former everyday condition
was a waking dream, an illusion.

- Rod Bucknell

If there were no illusion,
there would be no enlightenment.

- Eckhart Tolle

Without a problem
how can there be freedom?
Without conflict how can there be peace?
Without tension how can you know relaxation?

Some people change jobs, mates, and friends,
but never think of changing themselves.

Change - real change -
comes from the inside out.
It doesn't come from hacking at the leaves
of attitude and behaviour
with quick-fix techniques.
It comes from striking at the root - the fabric of
our thought, the fundamental, essential
paradigms, which give definition to our
character and create the lens
through which we see the world.

- Stephen Covey

The world would mould men
by changing their environment.
Christ changes men,
who then change their environment.
The world would shape human behaviour,
but Christ can change human nature.

- Ezra Taft Benson

God grant me the serenity
to accept the things I cannot change,
the courage to change the things I can,
and the wisdom to know the difference.

- Reinhold Niebuhr

If one desires a change,
one must be that change
before that change can take place.

- Gita Bellin

We must be the change we wish
to see in the world.

- Mahatma Gandhi

You can't step into the same river twice.
And it isn't just the river that's changed.

- Robert Allen

The only thing that is constant is change.

- Heracleitus

Everything that has a beginning has an ending.
Make your peace with that and all will be well.

- The Buddha

Earth brings us to life and nourishes us.
Earth takes us back again.
Birth and death are present in every moment.

- Thich Nhat Hanh

Once the game is over, the king and the pawn
go back into the same box.

- Italian proverb

Among all the uncertainties of life
there is one thing we can be sure of:
We won't be getting out of here alive!

Death is a reminder that we are alive.

He who has nothing to die for
has nothing to live for.

- Moroccan proverb

The mark of the immature man is
that he wants to die nobly for a cause,
while the mark of the mature man is
that he wants to live humbly for one.

- Wilhelm Stekel

Live as if you were to die tomorrow.
Learn as if you were to live for ever.

- Mahatma Gandhi

Life is no brief candle for me.
It is a sort of splendid torch which I have got
hold of for the moment and I want to make it
burn as brightly as possible before handing it on
to future generations.

- George Bernard Shaw

Life is a symphony which most of us
fail to play to the end.

He who lives in the present lives in eternity.

- Ludwig Wittgenstein

In the presence of eternity,
the mountains are as transient as the clouds.

- Robert Green Ingersoll

We need to find a path,
not to go from here to there,
but to go from here to here.

- Jakusho Kwong

The entire material-world journey
is all in that microscopic drop of a seedling
called our conception.
It came from *no-where*,
shows up in the *now-here*,
and is heading back to *no-where*.

- Wayne Dyer

I seek the truth everywhere,
and respect it when I find it,
and I submit to it whenever it is shown to me.

- Frederick the Great

Men stumble over the truth from time to time,
but most pick themselves up and hurry off
as if nothing had happened.

- Winston Churchill

There are no new truths,
but only truths that have not been recognised.

- Mary McCarthy

You cannot change the truth,
but the truth can change you.

There are three truths:
my truth, your truth, and the truth.

- Chinese proverb

Faith and reason are like two wings
on which the human spirit
rises to the contemplation of truth.

- John Paul II

The world says seeing is believing,
but faith says believing is seeing.

- Aristotle

It is not miracles that generate faith,
but faith that generates miracles.

- Fyodor Dostoevsky

Miracles are not contrary to nature,
but only contrary to
what we know about nature.

- Augustine

A miracle cannot prove what is impossible;
it is useful only to confirm what is possible.

- Maimonides

There are only two ways to live your life.
One is as though nothing is a miracle;
the other is as though everything is a miracle.

- Albert Einstein

Accept what comes to you totally and
completely so that you can appreciate it,
learn from it, and then let it go.

- Deepak Chopra

A thing is complete when you can let it be.

- *Gita Bellin*

It is the mark of an educated mind to be able
to entertain a thought without accepting it.

A great many people think they are thinking
when they are merely
rearranging their prejudices.

- *William James*

A man is getting along the road to wisdom
when he begins to realise
that his opinion is just an opinion.

I do not agree with what you say, but I will
defend to the death your right to say it.

- *Voltaire*

Those who know don't speak,
those who speak don't know.

- Lao Tzu

The more I know,
the more I realise I don't know.

- Albert Einstein

Strange how much you need to know
before you know how little you know.

You realise how little you know
when a child begins to ask questions.

- Robert Allen

I asked a child, walking with a candle,
'Where does the light come from?'
Instantly he blew it out. 'Tell me where it's
gone and I'll tell you where it came from.'

- Hasan of Basra

I find television very educational.
Every time someone switches it on,
I go into another room and read a good book.

- Groucho Marx

We have two ears and one mouth. We should
spend twice as much time listening as talking.

Listen or thy words will keep thee deaf.

- American Indian proverb

No one means all they say,
and very few say all they mean.

- David Baird

Tact is the art of thinking all you say
and not saying all you think.

Better to remain silent and be thought a fool,
than to speak and remove all doubt.

- Abraham Lincoln

If ignorance is bliss,
why aren't there more happy people?

Common sense is not so common.

- Voltaire

Knowledge without wisdom
is a load of books on the back of a donkey.

- Japanese proverb

You don't write a book because
you want to say something;
you write it because you have something to say.

- F. Scott Fitzgerald

You cannot drink the word 'water'.
The formula H_2O cannot float a ship.
The word 'rain' cannot get you wet.
You must experience water or rain to truly
know what the words mean. ... Words are only
meant to lead to the direct experience.

- Wayne Dyer

Everything you need to know is there;
it is just a matter of tuning in to it.

Wisdom is to know the harmony of things,
and joy is to dance to its rhythm.

My life is my message.

- Mahatma Gandhi

It is no use walking anywhere to preach
unless our walking is our preaching.

- Francis of Assisi

After all is said and done,
more is said than done.

There are no passengers on Spaceship Earth.
We are all crew.

- Marshall McLuhan

Think globally, act locally.

If you poison the environment,
the environment will poison you.

- Tony Follari

There is an inner ecology that relies
on the same principles of balance and holism
that create a healthy environment.

He that plants trees loves others beside himself.

- Thomas Fuller

The true meaning of life is to plant trees
under whose shade you do not expect to sit.

- Nelson Henderson

Love

and

Relationships

Love is the most powerful and
still the most unknown energy of the world.

- Pierre Teilhard de Chardin

And now abideth faith, hope, love, these three;
but the greatest of these is love.

- I Corinthians 13:13

If I have the gift of prophecy and can fathom
all mysteries and all knowledge,
and if I have a faith that can move mountains,
but have not love, I am nothing.

- I Corithians 13:2

Love conquers all things;
let us too surrender to love.

- Virgil

Love is best kept by giving it away.

You can't give away what you don't have.

- Wayne Dyer

Kindness is difficult to give away,
because the more you give,
the more it comes back to you.

Love cures people, the ones who receive love
and the ones who give it.

- Karl A. Menniger

A baby is born with a need to be loved -
and never outgrows it.

- Frank Clark

A loving person lives in a loving world.
A hostile person lives in a hostile world.
Everyone you meet is your mirror.

- Ken Keyes

Compassion for others begins with
kindness to ourselves.

- Pema Chodron

How can you accept others
if you cannot accept yourself?
How can you love others
if you do not love yourself?

People need loving the most
when they deserve it the least.

- John Harrigan

The only way to have a friend
is to be one.

- Ralph Waldo Emerson

You can make more friends by becoming
interested in other people
than by trying to get other people
interested in you.

- Dale Carnegie

No one cares how much you know,
until they know how much you care.

- Don Swartz

My best friend is the one
who brings out the best in me.

- Henry Ford

A friend is someone who reaches for your hand
and touches your heart.

Friendship is a journey
into the hearts of each other.

- Indian saying

A friend is someone who knows the song
in your heart and can sing it back to you
when you have forgotten the words.

- Donna Roberts

Some people come into our lives
and quickly go. Some stay for a while
and leave footprints on our hearts.
And we are never the same again.

The best mirror is an old friend.

- George Herbert

The best kind of friend is the kind you can sit
on a porch swing with, never say a word,
then walk away feeling like that was
the best conversation you've ever had.

My friend is one who takes me for who I am.

- Henry David Thoreau

A friend is someone with whom
you dare to be yourself.

- Frank Crane

A friend is someone who sees through you
and still enjoys the view.

- Wilma Askinas

Your friend is the man who
knows all about you, and still likes you.

- Elbert Hubbard

You can always tell a real friend.
When you've made a fool of yourself,
he doesn't feel you've done a permanent job.

- Lawrence J. Peter

The finest kind of friendship is between people
who expect a great deal of each other
but never ask it.

- Sylvia Bremer

No man can be happy without a friend,
nor be sure of his friend till he is unhappy.

- Thomas Fuller

Truly great friends are hard to find,
difficult to leave, and impossible to forget.

- G. Randolf

He can hardly be a true friend to another,
who is an enemy to himself.

- James Howell

We must be as careful to keep friends
as to make them.

- Lord Avebury

I grieve the loss of old friends,
only to find comfort in the love of new friends.

- *Glen Herrington-Hall*

A real friend is one who walks in
when the rest of the world walks out.

- *Walter Winchell*

When it's too painful to look back
and too frightening to look forward,
look beside you; a friend will be there.

We are not here to see through one another.
We are here to see one another through.

- *Carol Matthau*

To the world you may be just one person,
but to one person you may be the world.

In relationships you must make deposits of trust
before taking withdrawals.

Celebrate every relationship you've ever had.
For better or worse,
your relationships are your best teachers.

- Christiane Northrup

If you can learn from every relationship
and understand how it came into your life,
then no relationship needs to be
remembered with regret.

- Deepak Chopra

The quality of your life
is the quality of your relationships.

- Anthony Robbins

Most people enter into relationships with an eye
toward what they can get out of them,
rather than what they can put into them.

- Neale D. Walsch

Love is composed of a single soul
inhabiting two bodies.

- Aristotle

Love does not consist of gazing at each other,
but in looking outward together
in the same direction.

- Antoine de Saint-Exupery

The first duty of love is to listen.

- Paul Tillich

I love you, not only for what you are,
but for what I am with you.

- Roy Croft

Do you love me because I am beautiful,
or am I beautiful because you love me?

- Cinderella

Nobody is perfect
until you fall in love with them.

Falling in love is exactly that.
Falling.
You don't have any control over it.

We come to love
not by finding a perfect person,
but by learning to see
an imperfect person perfectly.

- Sam Keen

A successful marriage requires falling in love
many times, always with the same person.

- Mignon McLaughlin

Success in marriage is more than
finding the right person.
It is being the right person.

When I eventually met Mr Right,
I had no idea that his first name was Always.

- Rita Rudner

Don't wait for the one you can live with;
wait for the one you can't live without.

Be as enthusiastic to stay married
as you were to get married.

By all means marry.
If you get a good wife, you'll be happy.
If you get a bad one,
you'll become a philosopher ...
and that is a good thing for any man.

- Socrates

We are not here to be understood,
but to understand.
We are not here to be forgiven,
but to forgive.
We are not here to be loved,
but to love.

- Francis of Assisi

You will love it
because you will understand it.

- A Course in Miracles

Understanding:
the shortest distance between two people.

- Indian saying

There are hundreds of languages in the world,
but a smile speaks them all.

No smile is more beautiful
than the one that struggles through tears.

What do you do when the only person
who can make you stop crying
is the one who makes you cry?

Forgiveness:
The scent left by the rose,
on the heel that has crushed it.

- Mark Twain

Forgiveness of the present is even more
important than forgiveness of the past.

- Eckhart Tolle

Forgiveness is the most powerful thing you can
do for yourself on the spiritual path.
If you can't learn to forgive, you can forget
about getting to higher levels of awareness.

- Wayne Dyer

He who forgives ends the quarrel.

- African proverb

To err is human, to forgive divine.

- *Alexander Pope*

If you judge people,
you have no time to love them.

- *Mother Teresa*

When you judge another,
you do not define them; you define yourself
as someone who needs to judge.

- *Wayne Dyer*

My judgments prevent me from
seeing the good that lies beyond appearances.

- *Wayne Dyer*

When you meet a man,
you judge him by his clothes;
when you leave, you judge him by his heart.

- Russian proverb

To carry a grudge is like
being stung to death by one bee.

- William H. Walton

If bitten by a snake,
don't try to chase and kill it.
When someone strikes out at you verbally,
don't get upset and strike back, or the poison
will spread throughout your system.

To be wronged is nothing,
unless you continue to remember it.

- Confucius

You never get ahead of anyone
as long as you try to get even with them.

Understand that by trying to control others you
are actually putting yourself under their control.

- Lynn Champion

You can't hold a man down
without staying down with him.

- Booker T. Washington

A Native American elder once described his
own inner struggles in this manner:
'Inside of me there are two dogs
fighting each other.
One of the dogs is mean and evil, filled with
anger, hatred, bitterness, and revenge.
The other dog is good, filled with love,
kindness, compassion, and forgiveness.'
When asked which dog wins, he reflected for a
moment and replied, 'The one I feed the most.'

- George Bernard Shaw

When faced with the choice
of being 'right' or being 'kind',
choose the kind option every time.

- Wayne Dyer

It is nice to be important,
but it is more important to be nice.

- Morrie Field

Hate is like acid.
It can damage the vessel in which it is stored as
well as destroy the object on which it is poured.

- Ann Landers

Hating people is like burning down your own
house to get rid of a rat.

- Harry E. Fosdick

I have decided to stick with love.
Hate is too great a burden to bear.

- Martin Luther King

Hatred never ceases through hatred.
Only through love does hatred cease.

- The Buddha

Whoever gossips to you will gossip about you.

- Spanish proverb

Don't talk about yourself;
it will be done when you leave.

- Wilson Mizner

Praise in public. Correct in private.

Who you are speaks so loudly
I can't hear what you're saying.

- Ralph Waldo Emerson

If we could read
the secret history of our enemies,
we should find in each man's life sorrow and
suffering enough to disarm all hostility.

- Henry Wadsworth Longfellow

Let me walk three weeks in the footsteps of my enemy, carry the same burden, have the same trials as he, before I say one word to criticise.

Instead of putting others in their place, put yourself in their place.

I don't like that man.
I must get to know him better.

- Abraham Lincoln

Everything that irritates us about others can lead us to an understanding of ourselves.

When you see a good man, try to be like him.
When you see an evil man,
look for his errors within yourself.

- Confucius

No matter how bad your situation is,
you can always lose your temper
and make it worse.

- Indian saying

The best remedy for a short temper
is a long walk.

- Jacqueline Schiff

He who angers you conquers you.

- Elizabeth Kenny

People with clenched fists cannot shake hands.

- Indira Gandhi

The worst prison is a closed heart.

- John Paul II

The door to the human heart can be opened
only from the inside.

- Kathy Wagoner

There is no better exercise for the heart
than reaching down and lifting people up.

- John Andrew Holmes

In a full heart there is room for everything,
and in an empty heart there is room for nothing.

- Antonio Porchia

People catch our spirit like they catch our colds
- by getting close to us.

I myself am not able to visit all the sick,
the imprisoned, the suffering,
but I ask them to be close to me in spirit.

- John Paul II

Grief can take care of itself,
but to get the full value of joy
you must have somebody to divide it with.

- Mark Twain

Shared joy is a double joy;
shared sorrow is half a sorrow.

- Swedish proverb

Thousands of candles can be lit
from a single candle,
and the life of that candle will not be shortened.
Happiness never decreases by being shared.

- The Buddha

If you want others to be happy,
practise compassion.
If you want to be happy yourself,
practise compassion.

- 14th Dalai Lama

A little bit of fragrance always clings
to the hand that gives you roses.

- Chinese proverb

God said to a rabbi, 'I will show you hell.'
God showed him a room containing a pot of
delicious stew, surrounded by
famished, desperate people.
They held spoons with handles so long they
could not get the stew into their mouths.
'Now I will show you heaven', God said, and
showed him an identical room, with an identical
pot of stew and people holding identical spoons.
But they were well-nourished and happy.
'You see', God said,
'they have learned to feed one another.'

- Medieval Jewish story

Working together works!

Dependent people need others,
to get what they want.
Independent people can get what they want
through their own effort.
Interdependent people combine
their own efforts with the efforts of others
to achieve their greatest success.

- Stephen Covey

United we stand, divided we fall.

- Aesop

Men of quality are not afraid of
women for equality.

Service is not a big thing;
it is a lot of little things.

We make a living by what we get,
but we make a life by what we give.

- Winston Churchill

He who gives to me teaches me to give.

- Danish proverb

Don't judge each day by the harvest you reap
but by the seeds you plant.

- Robert Louis Stevenson

Do not do to others what you would
not wish them to do to you.

- Confucius

If you really want approval,
stop thinking about yourself, and
focus on reaching out and helping others.

- Wayne Dyer

The greatest good you can do for another
is not just to share your riches,
but to reveal to him his own.

- Benjamin Disraeli

There are two ways of spreading light:
to be the candle or the mirror that reflects it.

- Edith Wharton

We cannot hold a torch to light another's path
without brightening our own.

- Ben Sweetland

It is one of the most beautiful
compensations of this life
that no man can sincerely try to help another
without helping himself.

- Ralph Waldo Emerson

When an elderly woman was asked
why she was standing in line to buy stamps
from a teller when she could have
used a stamp machine, she replied:
'The machine won't ask me about my arthritis!'

You can't live a perfect day
without doing something for someone
who will never be able to repay you.

- John Wooden

The greatest pleasure I know is
to do a good action by stealth,
and to have it found out by accident.

- Charles Lamb

I expect to pass through this world but once;
any good thing, therefore, that I can do, or any
kindness that I can show to any fellow creature,
let me do it now; let me not defer or neglect it,
for I shall not pass this way again.

- Etienne de Grellet

You cannot do a kindness too soon because you
never know how soon it will be too late.

- Ralph Waldo Emerson

In a bus sat an old man clasping a bunch of
fresh flowers, and across the aisle was
a young girl, who kept eyeing the flowers.
Standing up to get off the bus, the old man
thrust the flowers into the girl's lap and said:
'I can see you love the flowers.
I'll tell my wife I gave them to you.'
The girl watched as he left the bus and walked
through the gate of a small cemetery.

- Bennet Cerf

God bless you.

NAMASTE:

I celebrate the place in you
where we are all one.

EAV..

Eskandar de Vos